The Writer's Creative Workbook

The WRITER'S Creative WORKBOOK

Finding your voice, embracing the page

JOY KENWARD

Illustrated by

RUTH ALLEN

Leaping Hare Press

First published in the UK in 2019 by
Leaping Hare Press
An imprint of The Quarto Group
The Old Brewery, 6 Blundell Street
London N7 9BH, United Kingdom
T (0)20 7700 6700 **F** (0)20 7700 8066
www.QuartoKnows.com

Text © 2019 Joy Kenward
Design and layout © 2019 Quarto Publishing plc

British Library Cataloguing-in-Publication Data
A catalogue record for this book is available from the
British Library

ISBN: 978-1-78240-890-1

This book was conceived, designed and produced by
Leaping Hare Press
58 West Street, Brighton BN1 2RA, United Kingdom

Publisher David Breuer
Editorial Director Tom Kitch
Art Director James Lawrence
Commissioning Editor Monica Perdoni
Project Editor Joanna Bentley
Design Manager Anna Stevens
Designer Wayne Blades

Printed in China

10 9 8 7 6 5 4 3 2 1

CONTENTS

INTRODUCTION

Writing may be a way of life for you, or simply something you'd like to do more often. It can be a wonderful way of allowing your voice to be heard—perhaps only by yourself—or of expanding that voice as far and powerfully as you wish.

This workbook is intended to help you discover and develop your writer's voice. It is set out in ten chapters, and can be used as a ten-session course, beginning with chapter one. Or you might prefer to start with any chapter that seems relevant to you, work through it at your own pace, then try another.

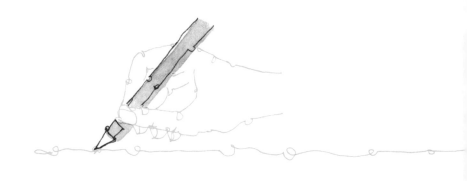

Some of the book is concerned with looking deeply within yourself to recognize your true voice and express it as a writer. Other sections deal with extending your writing using different methods and techniques, showing how you can express yourself in various ways to achieve a choice of effects.

Throughout the book you will find suggestions, prompts, and space for you to write. You will need a pen or pencil, and may also wish to have a separate notebook for writing longer pieces. There are examples which may help you, but it is not intended that you necessarily copy the style of the examples. One of my hopes for this book is that you will feel encouraged to develop your own unique style of writing, and enjoy the adventure.

Chapter One

THE WRITING ADVENTURE

Our pens are like magic wands—with a swirl and a dash and a few dots we create meaning through words. How wonderful! But this process is often easier said than done. As writers, we need to develop an awareness that is unusually acute: the touch of raindrops on our face, the scent of grass, the simple action of taking a breath. Such attentiveness does not exclude those who seek the lucidity of an articulate, thinking mind. On the contrary, it is through such conscious awareness that the writer comes to a clear understanding of their own abilities, needs, and preferences.

Stop for a minute and recognize how your feet connect with the ground at this moment. If you are sitting, notice the weight of your own body supported by the chair. Be aware of the air entering and

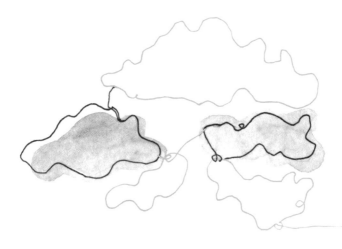

leaving your body as you breathe. Touch your face, or your hair. Notice the way this feels without judging or analyzing.

Similarly, when we write, we can try truly to appreciate the complete wonder of how our hand transfers thoughts into tangible, observable ideas—the reality of words on the page. So, the writer is a kind of magician, and the pen is a wand of power.

Take up your pen; become aware of its weight and capacity to transform. Think of the potential stories, poems, and other writings that will emerge from it in the time it will take you to work through this book. This is the beginning of the writing adventure.

My inner voice comes from

My mother's love, my aunt's laughter, the deafness and anxiety of my grandmother, my uncle's fearlessness, my sister's kinship, the logic of my father, the kindness of teachers, my nephew's smile.

My inner voice is shaped by

Memories of childhood, good times with friends, dark terrors, rescue and relief, first love, first heartbreak, loneliness, peacefulness, rage, the beauty of a garden, breaking my arm, the shade and sunlit shoulders of a distant hillside, snowfall, walking on a beach, this room.

A VOICE FOR LIFE

Through the magic of pen and paper our inner voices can connect with the world. Thoughts and ideas, stories and dreams spill in a stream from our pens. This is how the writer speaks in a myriad of voices, brought fresh from the imagination. A writer chooses which "voice" to use when he or she writes. In this respect, the writer always remains in control. But every writer has a true inner voice, essentially their own. Where does this voice come from?

Your own inner writer's voice has always been there, but, often, we try to copy others in the way we speak and put down our thoughts in writing. This is quite natural; babies learn to speak by copying others. As writers, we need to be able to use a variety of voices when, for example, creating the personalities of fictional characters, or presenting a biographical subject's tone of voice. But there can come a time when we want to ask ourselves, "Who am I?" In trying to speak and write only to please others, we can lose touch with our real self.

Our family, our friends, the places we have lived, our work, recreation, health, possessions—all these things establish and influence our thoughts and words. If, by gradual exploration, and by using this book, you find your true inner voice, remember that this is a precious possession. It will always be your choice whether or not to use it, but a strong connection with and knowledge of our true inner voice is a good foundation on which to begin the writing adventure.

Give some thought to your own inner voice. Where do you think it comes from? How has it developed? Who has influenced its tone? What knowledge has shaped it? What experiences or incidents have occurred to create or change it?

My inner voice comes from

My inner voice is shaped by

EXPLORING YOUR INNER VOICE

Through genetics and experience, we become who we are to the world. But who are we to ourselves? Very often, we don't really say the things we want to say. Even if we are known as great talkers, there can be a silence inside, blocking our real voice. People think they know us, but we may just be trying to please them, or to impress them, or to display a false cover in order to protect our true selves.

This exercise invites you to answer some questions about your feelings, rather than opinions or judgments. It will be helpful to be in a calm and clear state of mind,

1 Sit as comfortably as possible with this book and a pen or pencil in front of you. Put your feet flat on the floor if possible. Notice how it feels to have the soles of your feet connecting with the ground.

2 Turn your attention to your breathing. Notice the air entering and leaving your body; it's usually cooler as it enters your nose or mouth, and warmer as it leaves.

3 If thoughts try to disturb you, just acknowledge them but bring your attention back to your breath.

So that we can write with honesty, clarity, and joy, we need to get in touch with that voice inside. Sometimes it's buried so deep that we have to dig a little (but gently!) in order to find it. This is an exercise in exploration, and can be very rewarding.

The exercises on the following pages relate to your inner feelings, memories, and emotions. Because of this, it is best to keep your writing to yourself. This is because privacy can assist us in working out our true feelings. If others are involved, we will probably take their needs and opinions into account. And this exploration is just for you.

so that you are able to answer honestly without fear or analysis. Take some time to be gently in touch with that inner voice.

4 After a few minutes, place your hand on the open page of this book. Connect with how that feels, without analyzing or judging.

5 Pick up your pen or pencil. Feel the weight of it in your hand.

6 Now, answer the questions on the following pages. Take a calm breath in and out before and after reading each question, so that your answer comes from a place of clarity.

Which activities give you most pleasure?

Which place do you like best?

What is your favorite memory?

Which subject did you enjoy most at school?

If you could be somewhere completely alone, where would it be?

What is your favorite time of day?

What music would you listen to if no-one else could hear?

Who do you admire and respect most?

THE CONVERSATION

It is a great boon for fellow writers to be able to turn to each other for help. However, it is not always possible to talk to others when we need to, and not all writers are willing to share a writing project in progress, no matter how deep the difficulty. It is then that the inner voice is there to help.

Choose just one of the questions you answered on the previous pages. Now imagine that you are sharing your thoughts on that subject in a written conversation with your inner voice. This is intended as an enjoyable exercise. After all, your true preferences will also be those of your inner voice.

Write as if you are talking to a friend who shares your interests and passions. Ask this friend questions and then listen. Do you agree with the answers? Does your inner voice remember something you had forgotten, or recall some experience in a different way? Write down what you hear. Set your inner voice free with your writing.

Conversation with my inner voice

Next, it's time for you to hand over the writing entirely to your inner voice. Choose another of the questions, and write your thoughts concerning that activity, memory, place, etc. Try to write it entirely in the words of your inner voice, giving expression to any feelings of enjoyment, sadness, revelation, nostalgia, and so on, as well as any new thoughts generated by this exercise.

My inner voice speaks

THE CONVERSATION

Chapter Two

BEING A WRITER

What kind of a writer would you like to be? Do you know what would help you to accomplish this, and what stops you? Perhaps you are already an experienced writer, who feels the need for a boost to your creativity. Or perhaps you are a beginner, looking for ways and means of expressing yourself in words. In whatever way you have come to this moment in your creative life, it can be of real benefit to make a new commitment to your writing. As writers, we need to acknowledge the power in the way we convey our thoughts and ideas, and accept our ability to make a difference through our writing.

This chapter addresses the creative writer in you, acknowledging what constrains and inspires creativity, and suggesting ways of developing the writing craft by applying information received from our senses. By appealing to readers' imaginations in this way, they can experience what they read head-to-head with the writer, through the sense experiences that all humans share.

We can often feel tied up with tasks, responsibilities, and entertainments that call us away from our writing. This is one of the central problems for some of us who have the ability, imagination, and inspiration to write, yet can't seem to find the time. It may be the negative ego, telling us we are too lazy or dull to write, or it could be a generalized lack of confidence. It is worth looking at such drawbacks with honesty and compassion, in order to feel free to write.

One of the joys of writing freely and with commitment is to feel part of the community of writers who inspire us. Having dealt with our negative issues, we can return to our favorite authors with a new sense of connection and exploration, knowing we are now part of that community.

* A newspaper published a light-hearted letter I had written. People told me it made them smile.
* When a friend's partner died, I wrote to her from my heart. She told me later that this had helped her through a most difficult time.
* I wrote a poem that won a competition. I was delighted!

MAKING A COMMITMENT

We need to settle in our minds that we are writers. As such, we must give time to ourselves, to practice and express our voice as we wish. This is a commitment that might feel like a life change to those who have written little before, or who have felt that writing might be a waste of the time given to us to live our lives. But it's important to use our gift of creativity. The time we give to this is never wasted.

If you think of yourself as a writer, then of course you need to write. It does not have to be your profession. A gardener is a gardener, whether or not they are paid for the work. And using words effectively can be as powerful as planting a seed that grows into a tree. As writers, if we remember how our words can make a difference to ourselves and to others, this helps to boost our confidence.

Record some of the ways your own words have made a difference. If you don't have anything to record just now (or even if you have), here is a challenge: In the next few days, do some simple writing. Perhaps you could send a letter to a friend; email a politician about an important issue; write in verse or prose about an item in your house or garden, and what it means to you. Record here what you have written. It's testimony to your progress.

My writing that has made a difference

MAKING A COMMITMENT

In the examples below, the first sentence is really all "tell." The second sentence gives a fuller experience of the scene. Notice how the word "fresh" suggests the senses of touch and smell.

1. Rachel looked out of her open window and saw it was a beautiful summer morning.

2. As the sun rose over a garden in full bloom, Rachel opened her window onto the fresh summer day.

SENSING THE WORLD

Part of our commitment to the writing life is to practice techniques that develop our skills. But we should not become entrenched in rules and conventions. We need to learn adventurously and trust our original creativity.

The creative writer's rule of "Show, don't Tell" refers to allowing the reader to experience a scene, rather than just being told what is happening. For this, we need to acknowledge the five senses of sight, hearing, touch, taste, and smell. Even in the entirely imaginary worlds of science fiction the characters can only understand their world through the senses. There are, of course, real and fictional people who have lost one or more of the senses; the others are then so much more vital to their experience of life.

We don't need to always religiously mention all, or even any, of the senses when writing. But certainly consider them when you're preparing to write.

TIME WITH THE SENSES

Stop and take a couple of quiet breaths.

1 Close your eyes for a moment and then open them again. What do you see? What is ahead of you, and what is on the periphery of your vision?

2 Concentrate on your hearing. Even in a quiet room there may be something in the distance: the drone of traffic, a clock chiming, the sound of your own heart beating.

3 What are you touching? Think about what you can feel even without actively touching—perhaps the air temperature, a breeze, the chair you are sitting on, some physical sensation.

4 Can you taste anything? Coffee perhaps? The lingering flavor of your last meal? Toothpaste?

5 Give attention to your sense of smell. This is often the neglected or unnoticed sense. Are there any obvious scents or odors around you? If not, cup your hands over your nose and mouth and describe what you can smell.

Using the space below and on the following pages, write your thoughts or favorite memories of each of the senses.

What I love to see

What I love to hear

What I love to touch

What I love to taste

What I love to smell

SENSING THE WORLD

A SENSE OF PLACE

When remembering a place or describing a landscape, the senses are particularly important. The sense of smell, which doesn't tend to be used very prominently in writing, in real life can carry us straight back to a place in our distant memory. Where does the scent of lavender take you; or mown grass; or freshly washed cotton?

When trying to recall a particular memory —a childhood picnic, for example—we may think first of the people, vehicles, games, and activities of the day. But if we really want to take ourselves there in memory, we can quietly engage the imagination and slip back into the bodies we had then: feel the grass underfoot, taste those sandwiches, hear mother's voice.

Call a place to mind. This may be somewhere you've been recently, or a place you visited long ago, an old home, or a distant country. It doesn't have to be an outdoor place, although the outdoors often provides more to recall. Try to take yourself back there. Invite your body to travel there in memory, along with your mind. Now make a list of what you remember seeing, hearing, touching, tasting, and smelling in that place. The list will act as a prompt for a longer piece of writing overleaf.

My name for this place

What I could see, hear, touch, taste, and smell there

A SENSE OF PLACE

Using the same title for the place you are describing, now write up your memory of it. Use your list of everything you remember seeing, hearing, touching, tasting, and smelling as a prompt, but remember, you need not necessarily include every item on it. The senses are a guide to the world you are writing about, not an end in themselves. Trust your imagination and creativity to use them where it seems right.

Negative attachments

* I was called a "dreamer," not a "doer" from an early age.
* I'm too busy with family, job, activities, responsibilities.
* I think I could never live up to my father's high standards.
* I'm too old/young.

Positive thoughts

* Being a "dreamer" is essential for creativity.
* Writing is important to me. I shall make space in my life for it.
* I don't need to impress anyone to sit down and write.
* My age is exactly right for the experiences and ideas I can bring to my writing.

WRITING EVEN WHEN YOU CAN'T

Many of us feel we have "a book in us." We're bursting with the creative need to express ourselves. Yet there are times when all this positive energy falls flat because we just can't seem to write down the words.

Surprisingly, we can be more attached to our doubts and disappointments regarding our writing than we are to the positive call of our creativity. Our poor opinion of ourselves can be caused by upbringing, education, experiences, or simply our place in society. However they originate, these negative attachments are like knots in the smooth thread of our creativity.

Let's stop for a time and view the events, personalities, and facts of our life that prevent us from putting pen to paper. As creative beings, we can use our powerful imaginations to convert negative attachments into positive thoughts. Giving time to this is a great preparation for the next stage in the creative process.

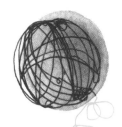

Write down any negative attachments that interfere with your ability to write creatively. Be gentle and truthful here. They may seem like a big deal now, but they are really just temporary knots in the creative process.

My negative attachments are

UNTYING THE KNOTS

No matter what our negative attachments are, we can still write. If we begin with true acceptance of any problems, they will lose their power. Please go back to your list of negative attachments on the previous page and write after each one, "And today I am writing." Then try the following exercise.

1 Take a deep breath, relax your muscles, and bring one of your negative "knots" to your consciousness. Be aware of its origin, if you wish, but do not waste time in judging its causes.

2 Accept that this is a problem. It does not need to go away, but you can withdraw it from the other things that matter to you. Put some space around it. Feel yourself inhabiting that space.

3 In the space opposite, write a statement that converts this negative attachment to a more positive concept. If this is difficult, imagine the problem belongs to a fictional character of your own invention. Write in the voice of someone who loves them and wishes them to succeed in their writing. This is powerful action.

4 Do the same thing for each of your negative attachments.

Converting my
negative attachments
to positive thoughts

Inspirations

* Maud, my grandmother, because she loved words.
* Mr. Lewis, a teacher who encouraged me.
* Carol Shields because her books are so beautifully written and are such absorbing stories.
* Terry Pratchett, whose writing is often very funny, but also gives wonderful insight into what it is to be human.
* Louisa M. Alcott because *Little Women* was a life-changer for me. I read it, wanted to be Jo, and decided to write.

THEY INSPIRE!

Is there anyone in particular who has inspired or motivated your writing? Some of us were encouraged by family or teachers, or were moved to start writing by attending a literary event.

Writing is of course a two-part adventure, because writers need readers almost as much as readers need writers. Most of us have favorite authors whom we would love to emulate, either because they tell an enthralling story, write beautiful prose, or touch our hearts in some way. These wonderful authors often provide the spark that lights the way to the life of writing.

Let's take some time to acknowledge the people who have awakened the writer in us. Writing their names connects us to them, and can have an inspirational effect.

Think of some inspirers and motivators in your writing life. Then, with your pen in your hand, think of just one of them, take a breath and imagine inhaling some of the delight you gained from this person's writing. Feel gratitude toward them, and write their name. Then add the word "because" and try to describe what it is about their influence, or their writing, that has encouraged or prompted you to write. Do this with each of your inspirers and motivators.

My inspirers and motivators

THEY INSPIRE!

Chapter Three

WATCHING THE WORLD

How do the writers we admire manage to engage our interest? How do they take us out of our lives so we can experience the world they have created for us through their writing?

The author Graham Greene wrote that writers have a "splinter of ice in their hearts," referring to their use of real—sometimes painful or shocking—experiences to give life to their writing. But if we were cold in our hearts, how could we express real emotion and real experiences in a way to which readers could relate? It's perhaps more valid to say that writers have a set of lenses in their minds. Some of these magnify, others are microscopic; some are crystal-clear and focused, others wide-angle. We look outward at the world around us; we look inward at our own physicality, at our own emotions and the way they interact.

It will enhance our writing if we can develop observational skills, free of judgment, and practice conveying in words what we experience via our senses and emotions. Through this practice, we can learn to write with authenticity, and express ourselves in appealing and original ways.

As we become more familiar with our true voice, as we look adventurously at ourselves and the world about us, we are becoming working writers. Take time to understand yourself as a writer, know what helps you to write, and respect your own ability to observe the world around you. You are creating the elements that will shape the worlds you are going to write, whether they are real or imaginary.

REMEMBERING EMOTION

A memory of excitement

I was only four, but I remember carrying a tiny chair out to the moving company's van. Rain was pouring down, but I didn't care. The excitement bubbled and rose and burst out of me in little, happy shrieks. Everyone was smiling. The driver gave us a lift in his cab. I remember the rain and the windshield wipers. But the glory of the day shone too brightly to be drowned out by any weather. I was four, and I was on my way to a new life.

Everyone experiences unforgettable times in their lives, times that are carved into memory and can be called to mind at any time. These might be incidents that mark a life change: starting school, getting married, losing a loved one, having a child. Or they can be events that happen when our lives appear to be moving at a regular pace. Out of the clear blue sky we fall in love, become involved in an accident, get into a fight, have an unexpected career-change, lose our possessions in a flood or fire. Any event like this is likely to have affected us emotionally. But can we put the memory and the feelings it generates into words?

Try to remember a time when you experienced a strong emotion—happiness, for example, or anger. Now try to recreate in writing how your body and mind experienced that emotion and the way it affected your actions and behavior.

My memory of feeling an emotion

WRITING THE SIGNS

When we see emotion in others, we often react with empathy; we smile because they look happy, or our hearts go out to someone who is obviously suffering. But it isn't always easy to describe in writing how we knew the other person's feelings. How would you portray the signs of grief, for example?

While it is perfectly valid to simply write "Leo's grief was obvious," the reader would experience the scene more vividly with an indication of how the emotion manifested on Leo's face and body. This would also provide an understanding of Leo's personality, based on how he displays emotion. Consider that people can show grief in many ways, from noisy floods of tears, to pale, shocked silence.

Snapshot of an emotion

She's walking easily, her posture upright, shoulders straight but relaxed. You couldn't help noticing her, even if everyone in the crowd wasn't standing back, applauding her. The look on her face is calm, pleasant, but her eyes are glowing, her cheeks just slightly flushed. And I think this moment, this very moment, is the time of her life.

Think of a time when you witnessed someone's emotion. Try to recall in writing what you saw. How did you know what they were feeling, and whether it was a positive or negative emotion? What was their facial expression like? What were their body movements? How was their voice?

*My memory of seeing
another person's emotion*

FEELING FOR THE WORDS

It's good practice to write out our memories of emotional times, although it isn't always easy to recreate the full atmosphere of the occasion. It is possible, though, to watch out for our feelings and reactions as we go through our day-to-day life. This doesn't have to be a cold process. On the contrary, watching ourselves with compassion brings self-understanding and helps us to develop into the writers we want to be. Mindful observation also helps writers to be aware,

What makes people, and fictional characters, react with emotion? Delayed public transport? Meeting a friend? Being robbed? Dealing with a fractious child? Write a list of real and imagined circumstances that would cause people to react with a variety of emotions at different levels. Remember that slight annoyance and great happiness are both emotions that can have physical signs.

without judgment, of emotions, reactions, and behavior in others. A wonderful by-product of this is that we learn to be more empathetic and intuitive writers.

Next time you feel emotion—whether a positive or negative one—try to "step back" from it for a moment or two. Notice how it feels in your mind and body. Similarly, when perceiving emotion in others, take a mental step back and (without staring) perceive how their faces and bodies react.

Reasons people react with emotion

In the next twenty-four hours, try to observe your own feelings and reactions, and those of people and animals around you. Then make notes about what you have observed. Remember you are not judging; you are gathering material for the writing life. When recording your observations, it is best not to name anyone, as this could cloud your vision and imagination. It's fine to give them fictional names.

Observations of myself

Observations of those around me

FEELING FOR THE WORDS

FEELING FOR FICTION

Observation of ourselves is, of course, a kind of research. We can use what we've learned about our own emotions and reactions to imbue our characters and their lives with authenticity. It could be said that we experience emotion virtually all the time, even if it's just a mild emotion like peacefulness or contentment.

An example of self-observation

I'm trying to do this—to write how I feel right now. I feel nervous. There's a tightness in my stomach; even a sensation of nausea. My head is kind of buzzing. My body is quite stiff—my legs crossed tightly, even though that's not really comfortable. As I become aware of that, I relax, uncross my legs, but not for long. In a minute I'm tense again. So, deliberately, I relax my shoulders. And I can still write while I do this.

Usually, any emotion we feel will have some effect on our bodies, and it can be interesting for a writer to be able to notice and describe this effect. Try this now, or the next time you are able to. Just stop and, for a few minutes, really notice your body and emotions, while trying not to consider the reasons for your feelings. Watch out for any small (or great) physical or mental discomfort, and feelings like annoyance, impatience, or curiosity, and notice how these affect your body. Write your findings in the space provided opposite.

How my emotions feel right now
and the effect this has on my body

A nervous subway ride

Jason sat on the New York subway train to Brighton Beach. He felt a fraud. His picture online looked a lot better than reality. What would that gorgeous girl think of him?

He realized his legs were tightly crossed. He uncrossed them, took a deep breath, noticing a trickle of sweat escaping from the thick layer of deodorant under his arm. He crossed his legs again. He had to try to chill out, or why bother to turn up for the date at all? Remember what Matt said: "Her picture's probably better than reality too. Don't worry, dude."

Oh no. Brighton Beach. Jason walked up the stairs to the ticket area, feeling as if he was going to vomit. There was someone standing under the clock. Long blonde hair, maybe a bit stooped.

"Are you Laura?" he said.

She looked up; big-eyed, nervous.

"Jason?"

He smiled. It was going to be OK.

Now, create a character who is going through similar physical and emotional reactions to your own. Try to make this character quite different from yourself, with their own reasons for feeling this way. On the left is a fictional scene, inspired by the example on page 52.

Using my own emotions for a fictional character

Chapter Four

GOING BACK

Our lives are the source of rich material, and it's well worth delving into them to find gems for enriching our writing. Some of us might consider our own lives to have been rather mundane, too ordinary to be of interest to readers. But every life is full of wonder. There have been people, places, and experiences we've known which have all had their fascination for us, and we only need to convey this in our writing for readers to be equally fascinated. When we practice expressing in words the full impression of our memories, we are developing skills that will strengthen the power of our writing.

In this chapter we'll be looking back at our lives as stories in their own right. Many people want to write their life story for their family to read, but it can also be a rewarding exercise in itself.

Our lives can be treated like fictional stories, introducing "bookmarks" that crop up from time to time and provide structure to the writing. We will return to the concerns of our childhood and our teenage years, trying to recall how it felt to be so young. We'll remember how important our pleasures and worries felt to us then, although we might since have dismissed them as trivial.

We'll also revisit the people we have known in our lives: people we haven't seen for years, people who shaped our lives, and others we live with every day. After all, our life story is not just the past, it is also the present, and what we choose to write about now.

BOOKMARKS

Writing about our own lives is a great way of developing writing skills. But writing a whole life story raises the question of what to include and what to leave out. We owe it to ourselves as writers to make it an interesting read. So, as with any narrative, our story needs shape and structure.

Structure can be provided in a life story by consciously including points of interest, or "narrative bookmarks" that occur and reoccur throughout and hold the reader's attention. These bookmarks could concern particular interests and activities, family, travel, health, or career. Taking one or more of these into account creates a pattern for your story. It will give perspective to chronological events, description of personalities, accounts of schooling, career, and more. The bookmarks might have their own narrative too, as an interest becomes a career, a problem is overcome, an ambition is realized.

Write a list of "bookmarks" that have occurred and reoccurred in your own life. These may evoke happy memories, difficult ones, or both. Be specific: for example, write "brain surgeon" or "sales assistant" rather than "my job." Don't give it too much thought; you will not need to use them all, and writing a list quickly can help to include useful ideas that wouldn't occur with too much over-thinking.

My bookmarks

If one of your bookmarks was "Writing," your first line could be:

All my life I've loved stories. The only way mother and father could persuade me to settle down to sleep at night was by reading to me, and then I would lie awake, inventing stories in my head.

For "Mountaineering," you might start with:

My first climbing experience was at the age of three, when my mother caught me halfway up the ten-foot-high wall outside our apartment building.

For "Asthma":

I cannot remember a time when asthma did not affect my life. In my first memory of it, I was sitting up in bed in the middle of the night, gasping for breath.

Next, write a "first line" (or lines) for each of your bookmarks, linking it in some way to the first decade of your life.

First lines for my first decade

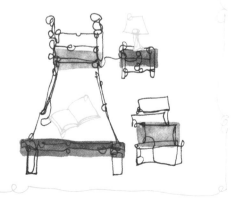

LIFE LINES

Look at the first lines you have written on the previous page, and choose one bookmark. It isn't that you can't use the other experiences for your life story if you wish, it's just that, for the purpose of this exercise, we are shaping your life story around just one bookmark.

Write down the bookmark you have chosen. Then, on the following pages, try writing a first line (or lines) for each stage of your life. This could be a line for each decade, or you could divide up your life in other ways (for example, starting school, going to college, your first home). Even if there is a period of time when your bookmark did not feature very strongly in your life, it can still be mentioned in its absence.

Example for a "Writing" bookmark

My first baby, Tom, was born when I was twenty-five years old. Because of him, and his brother and sister, my life filled up with the fun and chaos of family life. Writing seemed a far-off, nostalgic dream.

My bookmark choice

First line for stage two of my life

First line for stage three of my life

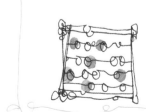

LIFE LINES

First lines for further stages of my life

LIFE LINES

AS A CHILD

Do you remember being a child? Most of us have memories from childhood, but when we write about them we are naturally writing as adults. We forget how small and vulnerable we were, how reliant on the adults around us for security and comfort. We forget the essential wonder small children feel at simple phenomena: raindrops on puddles, the taste of ice cream, a smiling stranger, bath water.

A child's perspective is not the same as ours; their eye level is literally lower. What they see is not quite what we see. Do you remember being a single child in a room of adults—lots of legs, shoes, and coats, and the difficulty of finding whichever adult you were with?

When we write about children, even about ourselves as children, we can try to remember with our whole mind and body what it was like to be a child.

Write a paragraph about your first day at school, or one of your earliest memories of school. What is the room like? How do you feel? Who is there? Before starting to write, pause for a few moments and politely ask your mind and body to help you write from the perspective of that little child.

My first day at school

ALIENS

Children grow, they learn, make friends, bring joy to their families. They develop very individual personalities, have their own preferences and interests. They face the light, full of promise.

And then: the teenage years approach. That beautiful child becomes sullen, beset by hormones, argumentative. When they speak, it begins to sound like a different language. Parents are baffled. They wonder

---

However easy, difficult, or exciting life was for you in your teenage years, try to write a paragraph about a memory of that time. Ask your body to help you remember. Waiting to write, take a breath and, for a moment, be that teenager again. Feel the memory flowing from your mind and body into your pen. Where are you? What's happening?

A memory from when I was a teenager

who took away their delightful child and left an alien behind—an alien who sleeps all day, eats everything or nothing, slams doors, and bursts into tears for no reason.

Do you remember? Was this ever you? Growing into adulthood is rarely easy. As with children, so with teenagers; when we write about them, we need to consider the world from their perspective—a world plagued by fears, the need to be independent, to rebel, to be accepted by their peers, even to be a child again.

PEOPLE

Let's go back now and meet up with people you've known in your life. Maybe they are friends you played with as a child, or old pals you still meet regularly. They could be family members you loved but who have died. They may be someone you didn't know well but who gave you encouragement or support which you've never forgotten.

When we think of the people we love, or who've shared activities with us, or been kind, or made us laugh, we rarely think of their appearance. This is a lesson for us when writing character. Appearance is not usually of great importance (although a particular quirk of clothing, for example a red scarf or tweed jacket, can serve as a useful "bookmark"). It's better if something more indicative of a person's personality is used to bring them to life. Perhaps they loved gardening, baking cakes, or watching soaps on TV. Maybe their house was always full of flowers. They might have chattered a lot, or been generous with gifts or time. Maybe their smile lit up the room.

Make a list of ten people who have meant a lot to you in your life. Some could be from the distant past, others could be people you see often today.

Ten important people in my life

1

2

3

4

5

6

7

8

9

10

When you've made your list of people, close your eyes for a minute or two and try to clear your mind. When you open your eyes, choose the first person who comes to mind from your list. Then, in a paragraph or two, write your thoughts about this person, the traits that illuminate their character, and any conversations, events, or experiences that connect them to you.

My thoughts about ...

Chapter Five

WORD MAGIC

We are writers; we care about words, and need to be selective and creative as we use them. Some words and phrases have strong meanings, yet this strength fades if they are employed too often, like a blade that dulls with overuse. The word "devastated," for example, has a powerful meaning, yet, if used to describe how a privileged and healthy child feels when she loses a toy, the original meaning of the word is weakened. It could hardly then be used to describe a child whose family and home are lost in a war zone. We writers need to be aware of this waning of strength when words and phrases are overused. It is not a phenomenon to be particularly regretted; this is how language evolves and develops. And writers are the people who keep language alive by constantly reinventing its use, refreshing phrases, and finding original ways of expression.

It might sound daunting to be in the forefront of developing language, but, really, it is the best fun to experiment with words. Imagine, at the beginning of the computer era, how enjoyable it must have been for the people who were naming parts and programs—"mouse," "spam," "blog," "software." They are all words that we use without thinking today, yet they had to be invented from scratch. You are certainly not expected to invent new words here, but to use these jewels of language in the most creative ways without changing their meaning.

So, we read, notice changes in language, and listen to the way people speak. We experiment with words, give voice to our fictional characters, and enjoy the process. But, we need to remember, even the most magical of words are there to serve the purpose of communication and creativity.

VOICES

As writers, we need to develop an interest in verbal expression. Listen to people talking. What do you understand about them by the way they speak? Can you estimate their age, or gauge their personality, health, or situation in life by listening to their tone of voice and the words they use? Would you be able to write dialogue in such a way that the reader would realize such things about your characters without being told? Think how a woman in her eighties might talk about her family, compared to a boy of fifteen. It is also worth remembering that the fictional characters we invent are not necessarily like us. If we decide to write in the voice of an eighteenth-century man of property, we wouldn't want to use the linguistic rhythms and idioms of someone raised in the early twenty-first century.

In the next few days, spend some time noticing how people of different ages and backgrounds speak. Please do not get too close and offend anyone by trying to copy down their words. Just be aware of details like tone of voice, pronunciation, and the actual words used by some groups but not others. This can be done by watching TV programs—then no one will be offended if you listen closely to their conversations! Make notes of the estimated ages and backgrounds and anything else of interest in the voices you hear.

The voices I have heard

Sample scene

Jessica (aged 33) is walking through the town center, on her way to the drugstore, when she sees her neighbor Nancy (aged 82). Nancy stops Jessica to tell her that there's a robbery going on at the drugstore. Their janitor, Michael (aged 22) comes along and joins the conversation.

Try writing a scene based on the summary on the left, using dialogue between all three of these characters. It's fine to use some narrative text—for example, "Jessica was walking through the town center"—alongside the dialogue. Use your imagination to decide how the scene develops.

My scene using dialogue

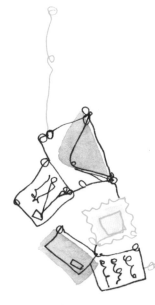

MORE THAN REAL

Metaphor and simile are widely used both in writing and everyday speech. A metaphor is the use of a word or phrase that is not factually true, but explains an idea or makes a comparison in a quirky way. An example of this would be, "That woman is a tiger" or "Paris is heaven." Similes declare something to be like something else: "He's as nice as cherry pie" or "I feel like a packhorse carrying all these groceries."

So metaphors and similes make what we say more than real, imbuing our words with color and significance.

One of the most famous metaphors is from William Shakespeare's play, *Romeo and Juliet*, when Romeo says, "But, soft, what light from yonder window breaks? It is the east, and Juliet is the sun." What lover wouldn't like that said about them?

Metaphors and similes

* He watched the sun rise in his daughter's face as she took her baby in her arms.
* That cake was an explosion of deliciousness in my mouth.
* His voice is like surf over gravel.

Try describing a scene, item, personality, or incident by using metaphor. Be adventurous, lighthearted, and experimental here. You might find your metaphors don't really work, or you might discover new and striking ways of description.

My new metaphors

MORE THAN REAL

PLAYING WITH WORDS

It's good to be playful with our writing. Life is too short, and writing too beautiful a subject to be taken very seriously. Too much seriousness sinks us into self-judgment and gloom. Trying out new metaphors is playful; using our own emotional experience to bring characters to life is playful; attempting complex poetic forms is playful.

Groups of writers who meet regularly often give each other fun tasks as a challenge. This could include choosing obscure words or an unusual theme for the next writing task. The result can be some healthy rivalry and a lot of laughs. If we take this lighthearted approach, we need never lose sight of our inner voice and creativity, which will take a boost from any writing task.

This is a fun exercise for the imagination. Here are two lists: on the left are adjectives, on the right, nouns. Pick a word at random from each list. This is your title for a piece of writing. It might be "trapped fruit" or "kaleidoscopic moon." Take a playful approach, and invite your inner voice to help. Be inspired, not constrained, by the random title. Use the following pages to write about three randomly chosen titles.

SPINNING	FRUIT
EMPTY	SUNSET
TRAPPED	FACE
FALSE	SPIRIT
COSTLY	MOON
SLOW	DRESS
FIRST	DREAMS
ALIEN	STORM
KALEIDOSCOPIC	MESSAGE
HISTORIC	DAWN

My first random title

My second random title

My third random title

PLAYING WITH WORDS

LEAVING IT OUT, FITTING IT IN

While we like playing with words, there are times when we have to keep within certain guidelines, whether we like it or not. We might be asked to write one thousand or one hundred words on a subject we are expert on. When this happens, we often have a lot more to say than will fit into the space. That's when we have to bid goodbye to some of our favorite phrases, or even a whole piece of information that at first seems essential.

Writers often make a point of reducing the number of words in a finished manuscript. This gives strength to what is left. For example, imagine a page describing a new character, their appearance, and the problems that presently concern them. Without the description of the character's appearance, their problems will have more focus, and be more likely to engage the reader.

Home, in fifty words

Moving to the city of Chicago was daunting. After small-town life, William feared he'd be out of his depth. But, stepping outside Union Station, he entered the tremendous life of the city like a captive fish released into the ocean. Hailing a cab, he smiled and thought, "I'm home."

A fun way to practice limiting the words in our writing is with the mini-saga. These little stories are written in exactly fifty words. They teach us not to waste words and to structure our writing carefully. You can use the space overleaf to write your own mini-saga. You probably won't manage exactly fifty words on the first attempt, and will have to change words and alter sentences before you succeed.

The rules: Your mini-saga must be exactly fifty words. Hyphenated words can be counted as one word or two—it's up to you. The title is **not** counted within the fifty words, but is limited to six words.

Use these pages to draft
and edit your fifty-word tale

CHIMES

When reading, try to sense the tempo of the prose or poetry. Feel the power of deliberate repetition, be aware of any undercurrent of emotion. Feel it with your mind and body, as you would feel a dance.

As well as rhythm, the juxtaposition of words, and any repetition of vowel and consonant sounds (assonance and alliteration), all contribute to a kind of "chiming" effect, like subtle music. We can also choose words to enhance atmosphere. For example, "branch" and "bough" mean almost the same thing, but the sharp "ch" sound in the former has a fresher quality, whereas "bough" provides a calmer sound. Sometimes, a writer seems to create prose and poetry simply for the sound of the words, like an artist in love with the sweep and flow of the paint.

Write a paragraph with a strong feel for the sound of the words. Don't worry too much about explaining your meaning. It can be subtle, embedded in sound and rhythm, not even obvious to you; an experiment in chiming.

Freeway

In filthy, feverish effluence, fetid
fumes infect my intellect. Shrilling,
shrapnel shreds of traffic racket
deafen and numb my mentality.
Jolting, convulsed, shivered
vehicles subvert my vision. But
overhead, overheard, over herds
of heavy transport—pressed,
corralled metal cattle—a blackbird's
liquid, fluting, leaping, pealing
rings of song swing out to another
listener, standing still and sanguine
on a hillside, hearing only as a hum
the far-off freeway murmur, mellow
as a baby's breath, threatening
nothing, only assuring, as the sure
ring of blackbird song, that the
singer, as the listener, still lives.

Chapter Six

RHYMES AND REASONS

We live in a world of sound and rhythm. Indeed, we rely on a regular, rhythmic heartbeat to keep us alive. It's no wonder we respond to the music of life and nature; the very planet we live on spins and circles the sun with beautiful regularity.

As writers, many of us feel sensitive to the rhythm and shape in language. And this isn't only in poems and songs. Whether spoken or written, words put together with a sense of pace and form can have a powerful effect.

For any writer committed to developing their skills, an insight into the rhythms and patterns of language can be provided by poetry. Even those who prefer prose can benefit from spending time with poetry; it enhances our writing by guiding us to use the right tone and pace for the atmosphere we want to create.

It's a good idea to try producing short poems to "punctuate" a writing day. Not only does this give us a break, it also freshens the mind, like cleansing the palate between courses of a meal. It works particularly well when we feel blocked with our writing, as it takes the mind off whatever project we're engaged in without abandoning our writing altogether.

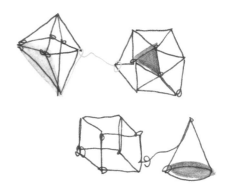

Generally, poetry produces its effects with fewer words than prose. In order to write poetry, we might have to think about structuring our writing within certain rules and conventions, using rhymes and rhythms. Even nonrhyming poetry without regular rhythm usually carries a sense of space and significance.

This chapter will introduce some traditional and up-to-date poetic ideas with exercises you might be interested to try. We look at the shape of individual words, rhymes, syllables, and stresses; find ways of intuitively converting prose into a poem; and dance with the music of words.

RHYMES AND REASONS

Example haikus

* We hated the rain
  But next day's puddles blessed us
  With sky at our feet.

* He left at sun-rise.
  It was day-break for the world,
  But heartbreak for me.

* She smiled a welcome
  From under her umbrella
  And rainbowed his day.

MAKING A POEM

There are so many varieties of poetry, and so many opinions as to what makes it "good," that it is really almost beyond definition. However, it is generally agreed that one or both of the following characteristics relate to most poems:

- Word patterns, including rhythm and rhyme-schemes.

- The most apt, concise, and original expression in words of emotions, experiences, sights, and so on.

It can be fun to fit our words into a rhyming scheme, or follow a set kind of rhythm, but it's important with poetry to have confidence in your own voice, and write what feels right to you.

An interesting but simple way to start writing poetry is with the haiku. These little poems can help us think about the structure of any piece of writing. A haiku traditionally contains just 17 syllables within its three lines: 5 in the first line, 7 in the second and 5 in the third. The lines are not usually rhymed. Haikus tend to be lyric poems, expressing feelings or emotions, and often concern nature.

Try making
haiku poems of
your own. Keep
to the 17-syllable,
three-line form
if you can.

MAKING A POEM

CELLPHONE

Call me any time

Everywhere I go

Loud and clear,
it will sound,

Linking me with
the world.

Perhaps it's
too much;

Have I become
over-reliant?

Other belongings
mean nothing;

Need of my phone
is paramount,

Every day, every hour,
every moment.

ACROSTICS

A fun way to play with words while engaging your creativity is to write acrostics. An acrostic is a type of verse where the initial letters of each line can be read together to make a word, which is in effect the title of the verse. Using someone's name as the title for an acrostic is quite popular; this could be used in a greetings card as an original and affectionate or humorous tribute to a friend. Whatever word or name is chosen as a title, it is intended to be in some way commented on or defined by the verse. Each line will generally not be very long, as acrostics tend to be concise.

Try writing an acrostic on the word "Home."
Remember that your verse is supposed to define
or comment on what Home means to you.

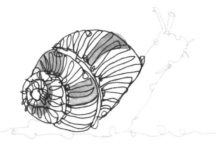

H

O

m

E

SIMPLE RHYMES

Simple rhymes are the best known of poetic forms. There's something extremely satisfying about reading rhyming verse, and even more so if we've managed to write it successfully. Rhyming poems, of course, have matching sounds at the ends of some of the lines. They also often have regular matching rhythm of various kinds.

Here's a limerick, with its well-known rhythmic pattern of two rhyming "couplets" (a couplet is a pair of successive rhyming lines, usually with the same rhythm), followed by a final line which rhymes with the first two.

> There's a clever young author from Utah
> Who creates movie-scripts on computer
> But prefers to compose
> With a pencil for prose
> While for history, it's quill-pens that suit her.

Even simpler is this two-line rhyme:

> A golden skyline marks a new day's start
> And warms the night-cold corners of my heart.

Now, try writing a short rhyming poem of your own.

FOOTSTEPS

Some poems don't rhyme, but have definite rhythm. Take a look at the extracts on this page: the first rhymes; the second does not. Read them aloud if you can, and notice their different rhythms.

Both use pairs of syllables for their rhythm. In "I Wandered Lonely as a Cloud" the pairs use a lightly sounded syllable followed by a strongly sounded one ("I **wan**dered **lon**ely **as** a **cloud**"). In "The Song of Hiawatha" each pair consists of a strongly sounded syllable followed by a light one ("**Bright** a**bove** him **shone** the **heav**ens"). Each pair of syllables is called a "metrical foot."

Making our own footsteps is so good for a writer. So let's go for a walk regularly, feel the rhythm of our own steps, and make poems out of them. The physical exercise will also produce endorphins that can help to spark our inspiration.

Different rhythms

I wandered lonely as a cloud
That floats on high o'er vales and hills,
When all at once I saw a crowd,
A host of golden daffodils;

from W. Wordsworth's "I Wandered Lonely as a Cloud"

Read the examples below two or three times, then try writing two four-line verses in each type of rhythm. You can use rhyme for the line endings if you wish.

Bright above him shone the heavens,
Level spread the lake before him;
From its bosom leaped the sturgeon,
Sparkling, flashing in the sunshine;

from H. W. Longfellow's "The Song of Hiawatha"

MAKING SPACE

Free-verse poetry has no regular rhyme
or rhythm. As an introduction to writing
it, we can divide prose into lines of verse.
In the example below, a paragraph of prose
has been transformed into a poem by
adding mid-sentence breaks and changing
a few words. Adding space introduces a
pause in the reading and adds unstated
significance, without necessarily having
obvious meaning.

Turning prose into poetry

Today, shoes clicking busily, I walk
down the road, loaded with bags
and boxes for the class. Something
stops me and I stand here, veiled
by my own breath. Quickly, like an
attentive servant, cold shawls my
neck and shoulders. But there's
a first daffodil in that yard, it's
Saturday and not raining for a
change. And I know I wouldn't
be in anyone else's shoes.

Shoes

Today, shoes
clicking busily, I walk laden
with bags and boxes for
the class.

Something stops me and I stand
veiled by my own breath. Quickly
like an attentive servant, cold
shawls my neck and shoulders.

But there's a first
daffodil in that yard.
Today's Saturday and
it's not raining.

Today I
wouldn't be in anyone else's
shoes.

Write a short paragraph of prose describing an incident or occasion. Then, on the following pages, experiment with line breaks and small word changes to transform your prose into a free-verse poem.

MAKING SPACE

Now create a poem from your paragraph of prose. You can add, change, or delete words as well as using line breaks. Try to work intuitively, remembering this is your poem, the meaning of which might not need to be obvious to others.

MAKING SPACE

Book:
A casket of pages loaded with treasures for the imagination.

Clock:
An innocent servant, carefully measuring my wasted time.

ORIGINAL CREATIONS

Originality is what all writers hope for. We can practice by writing short, creative definitions of ordinary things; these can then be used for writing free-verse poetry.

The best free-verse poetry is known for its originality. Unexpected spaces, metaphor, and intuitively chosen mid-sentence line breaks can produce meaning that suggests—rather than clearly explains—a theme or idea. A good example is "The Guardians" by Melanie Branton, which uses mid-sentence breaks, including one between verses that gives a sense of searching between the separated words "fingers" and "seeking."

The Guardians
by Melanie Branton

I use the names of people I love,
people who were once briefly kind to me,
as passwords, talismans I touch
several times a day, my fingers

seeking out their gentle kiss in the keys
to my treasure chest, my word hoard.
They stand sentry, ward off harm.
I type and, by the magic of megabytes,
they are transfigured into little stars.

I wish upon them.

Write your original short definitions of "friend" and "tree" on this page and, on the next pages, create a free-verse poem using one of your definitions as a guide.

Friend

Tree

ORIGINAL CREATIONS

Use one of your original definitions

as a guide and write a free-verse poem.

ORIGINAL CREATIONS

Chapter Seven

WHAT WE KNOW AND BEYOND

"Write what you know" is perennial advice for writers and "what we know" has featured earlier in this workbook. Our own knowledge and experience, as well as our powers of observation, allow us to describe the world around us, including the signs of emotion. When we write with authority about places we are familiar with or activities we are skilled at, this is as valuable as years of research.

However, "what we know" is never going to be the whole picture for a writer. Many of our activities and tasks are performed out of necessity, to earn a living or keep our homes in order. They are not always of great interest to us, even though we might be very

skilled in them. In order to spark true enthusiasm for our writing, we also need to "write what we love." There are often subjects, personalities, or distant countries that hold fascination for us, even if we might have no direct experience of them.

In this chapter, we'll be adding authenticity to a scene by lending our expertise to a fictional character. We'll reflect on the subjects that most hold our interest and consider how they might form part of creating a fictional story. We'll also think about the benefits of research and the importance of carrying it out on behalf of our fictional characters, and for the good of the story.

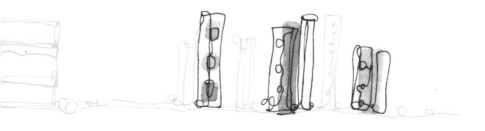

I'm back from lunch, feeling flushed, but nobody seems to notice. I go in to the counter area, hoist myself on to the high chair and open the blind. It's Mrs. Martin, paying in her regular check from her son. I stamp the paying-in slip. Blue ink, emblazoning today's date, 9.12.2019. And the ink is such a pure, deep blue, so much like the stain on that pregnancy testing stick, sitting secretly in the cupboard at home.

"Is anything wrong?" Mrs. Martin looks worried.

"No, everything's fine. I was just … just checking the date."

WHAT WE KNOW

We needn't live in exotic locations or follow exciting careers to have useful skills and experiences that add value to any story. The most thrilling or engaging novels are often set in ordinary surroundings and lived by characters with commonplace jobs or family life.

To set some pressing concern within the context of a person performing an ordinary task adds tension to the narrative. Imagine a character going through the motions of a task at work when she has just met the man of her dreams; or baking a cake after being told a loved one is dying; or cleaning a car as an earthquake begins.

Write a list of tasks and activities that you can do with confidence. Never mind if they seem mundane. Look at the examples on this page for some ideas.

Some ordinary activities

* Dispensing cash to a bank customer
* Clearing out the guttering
* Growing lettuce
* Singing every word of "I Will Survive"
* Driving a car
* Making lasagna

Check your list on the previous page. Imagine a fictional character of your own invention is performing one of these tasks when something is on their mind, making them feel anger, joy, pity, indignation, envy, or any emotion you would like to explore in this context. Write a short scene describing what your character is doing and how they are feeling.

WHAT WE KNOW

BEYOND

The things we love, are attracted to, and fascinated by are not, unfortunately, the means by which most of us make our livings. Beyond the work, society, and cultural activities of our usual lives we may have interests that absorb us, and which we have an aptitude to write about. Is there something you are good at but take for granted? For example, do you have a rapport with children? Are you knowledgeable about history, drawn to spirituality, fascinated by fashion? Do you spend every spare moment horse-riding?

You might be drawn to...

* Health and medicine
* Aircraft
* Elderly people
* Perfume
* Military history
* Baseball
* Home design and decorating

In a spirit of curiosity, spend a little time observing how you react to news items, articles, conversations, and what you see around you. Be gentle, watchful, without self-criticism. What we discover about ourselves and what we are drawn to—our "beyond" interests outside our usual lives—may be something we have always known, but not treated as valuable, or as a potential subject for writing. Without judgment or intention of any kind, write down on the opposite page the interests and passions you have observed in yourself.

My "beyond" interests

Choose one of the interests from your list on the previous page and relax with the idea of it in your mind for a few minutes. Then write freely about the subject. Why do you love it? How does it fascinate you? If somebody asked, what could you tell them about it? You don't have to answer these questions; just write what's in your mind about this subject.

THE SCENE

Any of your "beyond" interests could be an ideal background for a fictional scene. For example, if your particular interest is cars, you might describe a racing track, a car production line, or a driver of one of the very first automobiles. Indulge your imagination here. Your enthusiasm for the subject is worth as much as direct experience. Wherever you imagine the scene, put your mind there: feel that imaginary ground under your feet, scent the air, and look around you. Here is a character. Watch their movements. Are they at home here? Is the place new to them? See out of their eyes, inside their mind.

Special interest: Perfume

A scene inside a small, thatched building. On a wooden table there are dried flowers, herbs, resins, and small stoneware jars containing oil. A woman is working there by the light of a candle. She has something boiling in a pot over a fire. She is smelling a new batch of cooled liquid.

Write a short fictional scene using some aspect of your special interest. Include one or more characters, performing an activity relating to the subject.

Fictional special interest scene

CURIOSITY

When we have ideas for developing into
a story, we often imagine a character and
a scene. This could be as simple as the
short scene you have just written. It's at
this stage we need to become curious.
We ask questions. Some of these can only
be answered by researching the subject,
perhaps through the internet, reading
books, or speaking to people with the right
experience. Other questions can only be
answered by the writer—that's you.

The vital point to remember about research
for fiction is that it is only done on behalf
of your characters and for the use of your
story. For example, if you researched early
twentieth-century automobiles, it wouldn't
be appropriate to mention every detail
of design, materials, engines, and so on.
Instead, ask yourself what your characters
would see and experience.

On the following pages are some questions about
the short scene you have written on the previous
pages. Some will be answered by your creative
imagination. Others may require research.

When in history and where in the
world is this scene taking place?

What is the name of the character or
characters, and why are they here?

CURIOSITY

What more do you need to learn about your special interest on behalf of your characters?

How will you go about finding the answers?

The character has something on their mind.
What is it?

What happens immediately after this scene?

CURIOSITY

Chapter Eight

FICTION— ANOTHER WORLD

From time to time in this workbook, we have moved from our own experience—what we know and what we love—into the world of fiction. So now let's look more fully at the concept of fiction and what it means to us.

What is fiction? Answers can range from "imaginary stories" to "lies." But it's difficult to pin down a definition. Parables are fiction; allegories are fiction; historical stories that deal with real lives and real events are still classed as fiction. We often connect deeply and emotionally with imaginary characters in stories, and find philosophical, moral, and spiritual universal truths more meaningful presented in fiction than in any other genre.

We don't need a definition to enjoy reading fiction, and we don't need any excuse to enjoy writing it. Fiction opens up all the imaginary worlds we could wish for. They may be worlds very like our own, or they may be visions of entire fantasy. In the best stories, the reader feels they have been taken by the hand and walked through the world of the story, seeing and hearing it in their mind just as clearly as their own day-to-day life.

It can be great fun to create settings— wide landscapes, tiny rooms, oceans, forests— and to place fascinating characters there.

Welcome to wonderland.

A setting

On the high mountain pass, razor-sharp wind has been sculpting the ice for a thousand years. It has a terrible beauty, almost impossible for living creatures to endure, but there is a natural shelter near its top, a curved rock with a pillow of powdered snow, a possible refuge, a means of survival.

THE FUN IN FICTION

Having fun with fiction involves throwing over all our carefully researched information, concerns of scientific or logical balance, and worries about our ability to impress or meet the expectations of others. All these concerns are valid, but not when we're letting ourselves go and diving into a fictional world just for the fun of it. For this, we need to rest our "thinking and calculating" mind, and trust our imagination and creativity. This might seem easier said than done, so before you start writing take a few minutes to prepare with the exercise below.

1 Sit with your back straight, but as relaxed as possible, noticing the weight of your body on the chair. It may help to close your eyes.

2 Give your attention to your breathing and, while retaining a sense of anticipation, let your awareness turn away from the concerns of your mind.

Think of a place to set your fictional world. Where will you go? Is it a forest glade? A beach? A distant planet spinning round an alien sun? An underground cavern? A school room? Whatever setting you visualize, place yourself there in your imagination. Be aware of the atmosphere, warmth or cold, watch for movement, listen, feel. Write a paragraph about it.

Paragraph about my fictional setting

3 You are traveling into the realms of pure creativity on the flow of your in and out breath. Trust the process and the journey.

4 After a few minutes, take up your pen and contemplate the empty space on the page. Here you can create your fictional setting, using the questions and prompts above.

Now imagine a character appearing in the scene you have just created. They might be there already, or have only just arrived. Try to clear your mind for a moment, and watch for the character to appear in your consciousness, then write them into the scene. Your character should react in some way to the setting. What is on their mind? What are their thoughts and movements? And what happens next?

THE FUN IN FICTION

FRIENDS IN YOUR PEN

When a character enters a story, it's almost as if they have been born fully-formed, with personality, family, a wardrobe, and a whole life that no one, sometimes not even the writer, knows anything about. So, ideally, we would want to identify more closely with our main characters. It helps to write a "back story" about a character's life during the time before the story begins. This may include personality-forming events the character has experienced in their past, which are likely to be revealed through the finished narrative. Other parts of the back story will never appear, but help the writer to have a strong feel for the character's life and personality.

Create a new fictional character, or use the character you introduced into your setting in the previous exercise. Give them a name and create a short back story for them, using the headings on the following pages.

The name of my character

The historical period they are living in

Age and family background

Beliefs and interests

Wistful hopes
and/or burning
ambitions

Work or occupation

Important events in the past

Worries, problems, or concerns

THE INCIDENT

What makes real lives remarkable? What makes stories absorbing? The action that captures us as readers will be similar to what stops us in our tracks in real life. Whether people have experienced trauma, achievement, illness, good fortune, or tragedy, our awareness of it colors how we think of them. We're intrigued by mystery, shocked by violence, warmed by romance.

Such incidents or episodes can also be included as aspects of a character's life that took place before the main timeline of the story. Whatever occurred will play its part in shaping the character's personality. It may be mentioned from time to time, and will influence decisions they make or the actions they take.

Example of a character shaped by a past event

Tina lost a hand in an accident as a child. She's grown up coping well with this; she can drive and has a good, well-paid job. She sees that people are slightly shocked when they first notice her hand is missing, but she's used to it. Maybe at some point in the story, she'll tell someone how it happened.

Step back for a moment and feel the presence of your fictional character in your mind. Now think of an episode in their lives that happened before the timeline of the story. Write down what it was and how it affects their life.

With an hour to go before Aunt Winnie's arrival, Jada gazed at her spare room with a sense of horror.

An hour later, the doorbell chimed. Jada kicked a stray sock under the bed and dusted the little clock with her t-shirt. There were at least flowers in a jug and she'd remembered to add water. The bed was made with clean, if not ironed, linen, and most of the mess was bundled into a closet in her own room. She hurried to the door with a big smile on her face.

"Auntie! Welcome!"

WHAT WOULD THEY DO?

Like real people, fictional characters might be timid, neat, popular, moody, wacky, kind, or any of the hundreds of personality traits we could choose. It's good practice to write a scene showing your character performing an everyday or commonplace activity in a way that reveals their personality. This could be making breakfast, driving, or packing for a vacation. For this, we follow the creative writer's rule of "Show, don't tell" by describing the actions that show the trait. This can be further developed by writing a scene showing the character's actions when faced with an emergency or crisis.

Make a list of the personality traits you want to show in your character. First, write down the traits that would be visible when they perform ordinary tasks and activities. Then, list the traits that might emerge when they are faced with an emergency or crisis. These could be unexpected, or follow your character's normal reactions.

List of my
character's
personality
traits for
ordinary and
crisis situations

WHAT WOULD THEY DO?

Now write two paragraphs showing one or more of your character's personality traits. The first should show them performing an ordinary activity or task, the other how they react when faced with an emergency.

My character in an ordinary situation

My character in a crisis

WHAT WOULD THEY DO?

Chapter Nine

STORYTELLERS

What's your favorite kind of storyteller? Is it a "first-person" narrator—a character who appears in the story and relates exciting experiences to you face to face? Or do you prefer "third-person" narrative—a less personal approach, where the storyteller has wide knowledge and can see events from many points of view? Do you like the immediacy of present-tense narrative, or prefer a fireside tale of the past?

Readers tend to feel personally involved with a first-person storyteller who speaks directly about his or her actions and feelings. But, of course, these descriptions are limited to what that particular character can know. This might cause problems for a writer who wants to describe a scene, character, or thoughts outside the storyteller's knowledge.

The third-person narrator can see and hear everything in the world of the story, from storm clouds gathering over the South Pole, to thoughts within different characters' minds. This makes third-person narrative a less personal, but more flexible choice because, as well as allowing a wide-ranging view, it's equally possible for it to reveal only what is seen by one single character.

As writers, we choose our storyteller, just as much as we choose the characters who appear in our stories. The narrator's tone of voice, opinions, and how much they see and know about the unfolding story is our choice.

By no means do writers always use the same narrative style for everything they write; it depends how best we think a particular story can be told. This is often determined by our fictional characters: the main protagonist and others who assist, accompany, hinder, advise, and inspire her or him through the journey of the story. Trying out different styles and tenses can help create the atmosphere that feels right for our imaginary world.

I couldn't see anything because of the crowd of adults around me. Dad and Uncle Steve weren't taking any notice of me. They both looked worried. I think it was because of the game.

Emily could see nothing of the game because of the press of adult bodies around her. Her father and uncle were so absorbed in the action that they had temporarily forgotten the child. She looked up at their faces and sighed.

As Jones made the touchdown, the crowd roared and Emily's father and uncle lost interest in the child. With one minute to the end of the game, the Gulls were one point down. To have any hope of winning, they would have to attempt the risky two-point conversion.

WHO TELLS THE STORY?

How do we choose whether to use first-person or third-person storytelling? The examples on the left show three different styles: The first example is written in the first person, in the voice of the child, with her very limited view of the scene. The second example is written in the third person, again from the child's point of view, but in a more adult, authoritative voice. The final example is again written in the third person, but from a very wide, all-seeing view.

Write a scene of your own in three different styles: in first-person narrative; in a third-person narrative but from your character's point of view; and in an all-seeing third-person narrative.

Scene in first-person narrative

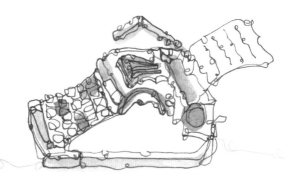

WHO TELLS THE STORY?

Scene in third-person narrative from character's point of view

Scene in "all-seeing"
third-person narrative

CHANGING THE WORLD

Can we make a difference to the world by changing our viewpoint? We can certainly alter a fictional world by doing so. If our story isn't progressing well, it can help to try rewriting it from a different character's point of view. Consider, for example, the story of Little Red Riding Hood. In the story, a little girl goes to visit her grandma in the woods. But the wicked wolf has eaten grandma and disguised himself in her clothes.

When the child arrives, she questions the wolf and is about to be eaten by him when a woodcutter rushes in and cuts off the wolf's head, releasing unharmed the undigested grandma. This is a well-known tale of alarm and rescue. But can you imagine it written from the wolf's point of view, or grandma's, or the woodcutter's?

Think of a story you know well, perhaps one of your own. Consider all the characters, including the minor ones. Now try to put yourself into the head of one of these minor characters. Even if they are a loyal spouse, servant, or parent of the main character, their priorities will be different. Write one of the scenes from this character's point of view.

CHANGING THE WORLD

Present tense, first person

Suddenly, the ground is sloping steeply; I'm struggling to balance. Underfoot, the rock is turning to scree. I slip, try to grab a bush. I'm falling.

Present tense, third person

Trying to keep upright, she doesn't notice the steep incline and scree ahead. When she slips, she's too near the edge.

Past tense, first person

Exhausted, I could hardly keep upright. I was swaying, slipping. Then my feet went from under me and I was falling.

Past tense, third person

The traveler was near the end of her strength. The path was treacherous ahead, but she continued in a haze of exhaustion, until she lost balance on a patch of scree and fell.

NOW AND THEN

Do we tell a story as if it is happening now, or in the past? Narrative in the present tense tends to have immediacy, a sense that the reader is very close to the action and can't guess what might happen next. Past tense has more authority, and can have a reflective quality, although some of the most gripping stories are written in the past tense.

It's worth experimenting with different styles to feel which is right for our work.

Take a few sentences from a scene you've written previously. Whichever style and tense you used then, try an alternative one now. It's not just a case of rewriting the scene almost word for word; think of yourself as a different storyteller for each style.

Scene retold in a new style

NOW AND THEN

TONE OF VOICE

What tones of voice do our fictional characters use in different situations? Their reactions, preoccupations, and opinions are aspects of their personality and will be reflected in the way they speak.

Tone of voice is as important for the narrator as it is for characters. Writers use an appropriate narrative tone, depending on the type of story we are writing. This would not usually be our own inner voice, but one of the many voices we learn to use as writers. Narrative tone can be very influential, notably in journalism, but also in a well-crafted story.

Narrative tone examples

The decent residents of Blue Creek neighborhood eventually got fed up with John Cooper's drunkenness and unsociable behavior. They taught him a lesson one night and left him in a ditch to cool off.

Ex-farmer, John Cooper, lost everything in the 2013 tornado. Deeply depressed, he became an alcoholic. Then one night, this once respected man was beaten up by hoodlums and almost died of exposure.

A family arrives in a new neighborhood. They pay to shelter in a motel garage. The woman gives birth there. On the following pages, write this scene in the voices of three different characters: The baby's mother. A neighbor who frowns upon homeless incomers. The motel manager who is glad of the extra rental.

The baby's mother speaks

The disapproving neighbor speaks

155

Chapter Ten

LOOKING AHEAD

Choosing writing as a way of life means that there is no ending to this curious, absorbing, rewarding, creative activity. When a writing project is finished, even one that has taken many years to complete, the writer will be anticipating the next story—the next beginning.

In this workbook we began by seeking our own inner voice, discovering our roots, and making a commitment to our writing. We've experimented with poetry, found the value in our own knowledge and skills, and traveled into the realms of fiction.

Now it's time to rationalize our learning and what we've created, and look ahead to our writing intentions for the future. Is it time

to make a plan? Do you intend to write your life story? Would you like to write more poetry, try travel writing, or enlarge on your ideas of fictional characters, landscapes, and adventures? Are you interested in biography, or writing about your expertise in certain subjects? All of this is a kind of storytelling, whether fiction or nonfiction, and there are ways of preparing the ground so that you can follow a clear path as you set out on your writing project.

Finally, but most importantly, we'll look at ways to care for the writer in us: to remember that he or she is a creative being and to explore the many ways we can provide nourishment for our imagination, and a regular infusion of inspiration.

WORKING TITLE

Many of us have always known what we want to write. Be it a novel, short stories, poetry, travel writing, biography, or any other form of writing, this is the time to clarify ideas you may have had recently, or which have been brewing for a long time.

Working title:
Oliver's dragon

A fantasy novel about a boy who discovers a small, lost dragon in his bedroom, and has to help her find her family, before humans arrive and put her in a zoo.

Working title:
Indian odyssey

An account of my six-month journey around India, offering suggestions and advice to those who want to take the same trip.

Working title:
Eleanor and Lizzie

A historical novel of Eleanor Roosevelt's life, but from the point of view of a fictional loyal servant.

Can you describe in a few words the writing project you are hoping to produce? To do so is a creative act in itself. You might already be certain what you want to call it. Otherwise, choose a simple working title. This will transform your plan into a real entity, not just a vague hope for the future.

Write your working title and a few lines
of description about your project.

Now ask yourself the following questions about your project. They apply as much to nonfiction as to fiction.

What timescale will the story cover (a year, a week, a lifetime) and what period is it set in ?

In which settings will it take place?

Who is the
main character
or person and
who are the
other important
characters?

What are
their problems
or ambitions
that feature
significantly
in the story?

TIMES AND SEASONS

When tracking the timescale in which your story takes place, an awareness of the outside world helps give life to the action. Check for important national and international events that might impact on your characters. For example, if your timescale included the year 2001, you would probably think it necessary to consider how your characters react to the events on September 11 that year.

When planning events for your story, think about the time of day, weather, and season. Creating an unexpected snowstorm, for example, can provide the event that causes two characters to meet. We all have some personal knowledge of weather events, although not all of us have experienced extremes of heat and cold, so will have to use research and imagination. This might include going out into nature regularly, which would also benefit our bodies and our creativity.

For practice, write a scene where two characters meet in extreme weather conditions. Imagine how it would feel to be in the scene, and ask your body to imagine it too: uncomfortable heat; rain dripping down the back of your neck; or icy, numb feet.

*Characters meet in extreme weather conditions
(very hot, cold, wet, or windy)*

TIMES AND SEASONS

Pace example version 1

Megan lit a cigarette and inhaled slowly. It was good to be on the beach again. There were a few children playing, their voices hardly registering on her consciousness. Behind their laughter and shouts, there came the regular thrum of a boat engine. Megan watched. There was something familiar about the shape of the boat. And then she understood why.

Pace example version 2

Megan stood on the beach, sucking a cigarette, trying to relax. Her eyes flicked over the scene. Kids playing, sun-topped waves; a boat chugging into the bay; all peaceful enough. But that boat engine, assertive under the kids' yells; it bothered her. She squinted into the light. The cigarette dropped unnoticed to the sand. That boat. She knew it.

PACING THE PAGE

We can use an appropriate pace for our writing according to the speed at which we want events to develop. We can regulate the pace simply by adjusting the amount of words we use to describe a scene. Generally, the more words, the slower the pace.

However, pace is also controlled by phrasing and by choosing words for their sound. The two examples on the left describe the same scene and events, and they have exactly the same number of words. But the short phrases and sentences in the second example contribute to the sense of tension that is missing in the first. Neither is right or wrong; it depends on the impression we are seeking. Of course, pace, along with any other effect, is never down to just one technique. We choose words, phrases, and sentences for their meaning, as well as their shape and sound. If in doubt, remember to trust your creative instinct.

Try writing a paragraph of your own, concentrating on pace.

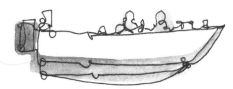

PACING THE PAGE

ENDINGS

There's something very special about endings. For a writer, it's often a time to celebrate and look to the future. But we writers need to be aware of endings throughout our work. We have seen earlier in this workbook how carefully chosen line endings can give a sense of significance in poetry. It's similar with prose. If we end a sentence, paragraph, section, or chapter with a particularly strong or atmospheric word, we'll boost its effect and set up expectations for what follows.

Different endings

The day was dipping into gloom, but little Ayesha, skipping along the sidewalk, was all happiness.

Little Ayesha, skipping along the sidewalk, was all happiness, but the day was dipping into gloom.

The examples on the left show how the meaning and mood of a sentence can be dramatically affected by how we choose to end it: the first sentence ends with happiness, the other with gloom. Experiment by writing some sentences of your own that end with different atmospheric words or phrases.

My evocative sentence endings

An important function of a story ending is to guide the writer. Often, we begin a story with ease, but can become overwhelmed by possibilities as it progresses. If this happens to you, try writing the final paragraph of your story, even if you've only just begun. This provides a focus, a point in the wide landscape of imagination to make for, even if you end up changing it later. The journey is so much easier when we know where we are going.

Write the final paragraph of a story, perhaps one you've already begun, or one you haven't thought of yet. This ending could lead to a beginning.

ENDINGS

SUSTAINING THE WRITER

With the commitment we've made to our writing comes the need to sustain and care for the writer in us. Here are six "areas of maintenance" that need regular attention.

* We are writers, and need to write. We feel unsettled if we leave too much time between writing sessions. Getting back to it helps us feel fine again.

* We need our voice to be heard, so we connect with our inner voice every day.

* We'll be cheered and encouraged by the endorphins provided by physical movement, so let's take regular exercise.

* We can be helped and inspired by our own writing talisman. Let's find an artefact or small object that reminds us of that writer in us, and keep it in a pocket or on our desk.

* We are part of nature, so let's take our senses into nature every day, even if just to feel the air and see the sky.

* We need a "stepping back" time when we are aware, without judgment, of our life's realities, and of creativity as an essential part of that life. So let's give ourselves that time every day.

The following pages invite you to consider how you can maintain and nurture creativity in your daily life. Write your response to each of the questions.

When shall I have my regular writing sessions?

How shall I connect with my inner voice each day?

How shall I take physical daily exercise?

What shall I use as my writing talisman?
Where shall I keep it?

How can I get into nature regularly?

When can I have my quiet,
"stepping back" time each day?

SUSTAINING THE WRITER

EPILOGUE

To be able to access our creativity is a great blessing. I hope this workbook has helped you to do so. Creative beings, especially writers, sometimes have doubts about their work. If you wait for a few minutes every day, providing space for your creative voice to enter, there will be no need for doubt, only joy. When we know what we love, the subjects that fill us with enthusiasm, and the skills that give a strong foundation to our work, and when we meet every day with our inner voice, reflect on others with understanding, and utilize the same compassion for ourselves, then our writing will bring new adventures every day. And, at our journey's end, we come back to one beautiful truth about the writing life: for every ending there is always a beginning, and this is probably more true of writing than of many other activities. We can always look ahead to a new story, new characters, new poems, a new world.

NOTES

Use this space to jot down ideas
to be used one day.

ACKNOWLEDGMENTS

I would like to thank everyone at Leaping Hare Press, who gave me the opportunity of writing this book, especially my excellent editor, Joanna Bentley, and the wonderful Monica Perdoni, who supported the idea from the beginning. Thank you to my friend Josie Rees for her help and advice just when I needed it. I would also like to express my gratitude to all the students and workshop participants through the years who continue to be constantly surprising and inspirational. I am indebted to my local Buddhist group for their teachings, and the Quakers for introducing me to their unique kind of active silence and adventurous living. Most and best, my thanks go to my husband, Bob Kenward, for his unfailing patience and constant support.